The 21st Century Mother's Guide to

MANAGING YOUR TIME

and Taking Control of Your Life!

By
Susan Tatsui-D'Arcy

Director and Time Management Consultant
at Merit Educational Consultants, LLC

Published by Merit Educational Consultants, LLC
P.O. Box 2988, Santa Cruz, California 95063

First published in the United States of America by Merit Educational Consultants LLC and Lulu.

Copyright ** Merit Educational Consultants, LLC, 2006
All rights reserved

Library of Congress Cataloging in Publication Data

Tatsui-D'Arcy, Susan, 2006
1. College advisory. 2. Tatsui-D'Arcy, Susan.

ISBN: 978-0-6151-3767-4

Printed in the United States of America

Except in the United States of America, this book is sold subject to the condition that it shall not, by way of trade or otherwise, be lent, copied, re-sold, hired out, or otherwise circulated without the publisher's prior consent in any form of binding or cover other than that in which it is published and without a similar condition including this condition being imposed on the subsequent purchaser.

Need Help? Visit www.meritworld.com

Table of Contents

Introduction 7
How to Get Started? 11
   "I Don't Have Time to Get Organized 11
   Three Things you'll Need to End the Chaos! 12
   Stop Using your Old Organizers/Calendars 12
   The Merit Planner 15
Start Entering Tasks in Your Planner! 17
   Keep a Journal of your Time 17
   Make a List of all your Tasks 18
   Today's Tasks 19
   The Rest of the Week's Tasks 19
   Fill in the Rest of the Month/Year's Tasks 20
   Don't Forget Important Dates 20
   Schedule for the Holidays 23
   Keep it Realistic 23
Planning Ahead for Long-Term Goals 27
   Start with a List 27
   Break up the Subtasks 28
   Enter the Times into the Planner 30
   My Success Story 30
   Sample Planner Page: Notes Section 30
Living by the Planner 35
   Consult the Planner Often 35
   Have the Planner Nearby 35
   Readjusting to Changes 36
   Highlight off Completed Tasks 36
   After-the-Fact Entries 41
   Didn't do the Task, Now What? 41
   Lapses in Use 41
Keeping Track of Family/their Schedules 43
   Add in Kids' Schedules 43
   Transportation for the Kids 44
   Carpool Schedule 45
   Carpool Schedule in Planner 47
   Coordinating with your Spouse 49
   Another Party? 49
   After-School Activities 50

Need Help? Call 831.462.5655

Time Management for the Family 51
   Hold a Family Meeting to Get them Started 51
   Start Them as Young as Six Years Old! 52
   Enter in Kids' Schedules 52
   Family Activities 52
   What about Homework? 52
   Kids Shouldn't Keep Lists of Homework! 53
   Scheduling Homework into the Planner 53
   Long-Term Projects for Kids 54
   Organize the Entire Year 54
   Social Time and Down Time 57
   Get a Copy of your Children's' Schedule 57
   Limiting Time-Wasters 57
   What about Chores? 58
   Sample Planner: Scheduling Time - Chores 59

Weekly Family Meetings 61
   Family Brainstorm Sessions 61
   Synchronizing Family Members' Schedules 62
   Plan your Weekends 63
   Coordinate the Shopping Schedule 63
   Plan Your Next Meeting before you Leave 63

Use Trays for Family Communication 65
   How to Pass Messages with Trays 65
   Make Sure Trays Get Checked Regularly 66
   How to Handle Requests in Your Tray 66

Cooking Meals 67
   Plan the Menu for One Week 67
   Kids Can Make Their Own Lunches 68
   Let the Kids Prepare Individual Meals 68
   Weekly Shopping List and Menu 69
   Meal Prep as a Family 71
   Meal Cleanup 71

Household Chores 73
   Delegate, Delegate, Delegate! 73
   What your Kids can do to Help 74
   How to Divide Up Chores 75
   Assign the Chores 76
   Rotate the Jobs 76
   Spring Cleaning Day 76
   How to Divide the Jobs 77
   Getting the Spring Cleaning Supplies 77
   Spring-Cleaning Day Itself 77

Need Help? Visit www.meritworld.com

Shopping and Errands 79
   Only Buy Groceries once a Week 79
   Use a Grocery List 80
   Plan out the Meals for the Week 80
   Driving Errands 80
   Take Advantage of your Commute 81
   Don't do it all Yourself 81
   Have it Delivered 82
Time for You! 83
   Schedule Time for YOU! 83
   Creative Time for You 84
   Time to get Perspective 84
Other Ways to Better Use your Time 85
   Review Planner Entries 85
   Don't be a Slave to Your Phone! 86
   E-mail is Fast and Effective 87
   Setting your Limits 87
   Need Extra Help? 87
   Limiting Time-Wasters 88
   Being More Efficient at Work 88
   Teach Time Management to Co-workers 88
A Word on Motivation 91
   Don't Go it Alone 91
   Think about How Much You've Changed 92
   Treat Yourself 92
   Kids Especially Need Motivation 92
Conclusion 95
Index 96

For Rob, Nicole, and Jaclyn

Introduction

Mothers today have a difficult and under appreciated job.

As a professional consultant in time management, I've worked with hundreds of mothers from all walks of life. They come to me for help with problems that are invariably similar: they're being pulled in every direction by the competing demands of their family, their household, and their career. They spend their days running this way and that, always feeling rushed and stressed. There's never enough time. Everything waits to the last minute. It's too early when they have to wake up, too late when they get to sleep. And for tomorrow they're only looking forward to more of the same mad runaround.

In short, their lives have gotten out of control.

I'm sure the story sounds familiar. Whether you're an at-home mom or you're a CEO, you feel the same

Need Help? Call 831.462.5655

Introduction

stress because you have a similar set of demands to juggle. Maybe you've even tried to get organized before. Maybe you gave up because the chaos permeated every aspect of your life and you couldn't even decide where to start. You're not alone. I can help.

In most cases, the problem of disorganization is caused by inadequate planning. Because you're always rushed, you never have a moment to sit down and contemplate all the things to do in a given day. You adapt moment-to-moment, day-to-day. The larger picture passes you by. Every demand seems like an emergency. But you have no plan that shows you how to utilize your time for maximum efficiency.

How do you break the cycle? There's no one trick. It will depend more on careful time management and on doing lots of little things to improve the way you use your time. For instance, many mothers waste time by running to the store everyday—but I'll show you how you can streamline everything into fewer trips. And many of us live at the mercy of our telephone—but I'll show you how to budget specific times for using the phone, so that you won't be getting interrupted anymore. These little things have a way of adding up to results that are huge.

Not only will this guide help you transform the way you live your life—but it will make the transition more manageable by guiding you through every step. First, we'll start with a time management program for you. Pretty soon, you'll have the time to relax again. After we get you set up and feeling like you're in control, it's time to start examining other aspects of your life. We'll set up the kids too, so you won't be getting any more of those panicky calls because you forgot about soccer practice. Next we'll look at household responsibilities, to make sure that dinner gets cooked and the laundry gets washed. With you and the home in check, we'll look at some other ways to save even more

Need Help? Visit www.meritworld.com

Introduction

time. We'll even make sure to schedule in the one activity that so many mothers miss—time for just you.

You'll be surprised at how you transform from a disorganized stress-case to a woman who accomplishes what she wants because she knows how to do it!

Need Help? Call 831.462.5655

Chapter I
How to Get Started?

"I Don't Have Time to Get Organized . . . I Feel So Overwhelmed!"

Disorganization works like a downward spiral. It is rarely restricted to just one aspect of your life—it usually pervades everything, which makes it that much more difficult to get any solid footing to organize yourself. But you need to start somewhere. Before you start organizing the physical clutter in your life, such as your home and your office, you need to start with organizing you and your time. There's no need to blow your money on stacks of books on organization and self-help, hundreds of dollars of storage systems, and all sorts of filing cabinets. In fact, these are only likely to add to the clutter!

How to Get Started?

Three Things you'll Need to End the Chaos!

You already have this book, so you'll only need three more things: the Merit Planner will give you the power to plan out every minute of your day. Next, find some letter-size stackable trays (although these can wait until later). You'll need them for your home and maybe your office. Get one tray for every person in your family, as well as for all your household help, such as your housekeeper, babysitter, pool cleaner, etc. Next you'll need a pencil with an eraser. That's it!

Stop Using your Old Organizers and Calendars

Your current system of organization hasn't been helping you get the job done, so it's time to get rid of it. Let's look at some of the problems with traditional organizational tools, before I show you why the Merit Planner is the most useful.

Most personal planners have two downfalls. You get spaces for zillions of lists, but the lists just leave you feeling completely overwhelmed and do little to help you plan how to approach actually doing your tasks. Second, these planners tend to give little space, if any, to weekends and evenings. Since most mothers stay busy on weekends and evenings, this gives you a lopsided view of your week.

Calendars let you schedule important dates, but they don't have enough space for scheduling many things on the same date. Calendars also aren't portable enough to be taken with you when you go out.

Computerized organizers don't help too much either. With any high-tech device, you inevitably waste hours troubleshooting the problems, overcoming the annoyances, and figuring out the bells and whistles. Then you have to worry because whenever the information is stored electronically, your life will derail if the system crashes. And your schedule isn't always instantaneously

Need Help? Visit www.meritworld.com

Sample Planner Page

Mon.,		Tue.,		Wed.,	
7:00		7:00		7:00	
7:30		7:30		7:30	
8:00		8:00		8:00	
8:30		8:30		8:30	
9:00		9:00		9:00	
9:15		9:15		9:15	
9:30		9:30		9:30	
9:45		9:45		9:45	
10:00		10:00		10:00	
10:15		10:15		10:15	
10:30		10:30		10:30	
10:45		10:45		10:45	
11:00		11:00		11:00	
11:15		11:15		11:15	
11:30		11:30		11:30	
11:45		11:45		11:45	
12:00		12:00		12:00	
12:15		12:15		12:15	
12:30		12:30		12:30	
12:45		12:45		12:45	
1:00		1:00		1:00	
1:15		1:15		1:15	
1:30		1:30		1:30	
1:45		1:45		1:45	
2:00		2:00		2:00	
2:15		2:15		2:15	
2:30		2:30		2:30	
2:45		2:45		2:45	
3:00		3:00		3:00	
3:15		3:15		3:15	
3:30		3:30		3:30	
3:45		3:45		3:45	
4:00		4:00		4:00	
4:15		4:15		4:15	
4:30		4:30		4:30	
4:45		4:45		4:45	
5:00		5:00		5:00	
5:15		5:15		5:15	
5:30		5:30		5:30	
5:45		5:45		5:45	
6:00		6:00		6:00	
6:15		6:15		6:15	
6:30		6:30		6:30	
6:45		6:45		6:45	
7:00	9:30	7:00	9:30	7:00	9:30
7:15	9:45	7:15	9:45	7:15	9:45
7:30	10:00	7:30	10:00	7:30	10:00
7:45	10:15	7:45	10:15	7:45	10:15
8:00	10:30	8:00	10:30	8:00	10:30
8:15	10:45	8:15	10:45	8:15	10:45
8:30	11:00	8:30	11:00	8:30	11:00
8:45	11:15	8:45	11:15	8:45	11:15
9:00	11:30	9:00	11:30	9:00	11:30
9:15	11:45	9:15	11:45	9:15	11:45

Need Help? Call 831.462.5655

How to Get Started?

available; you have to turn on the system and navigate the menus every time you want to check it. Since you'll be consulting your organizer several times a day, this wastes lots of time.

Handheld electronic organizers, such as Palms are sleek and portable, and they work best for organizing your contact information. But they work poorly for managing your schedule because they don't have the screen space to view an entire day at once.

But don't get rid of your old planners and organizers just yet. You'll need to keep them a bit longer so you can copy down everything you had previously scheduled.

The Merit Planner

Since it's all on paper, the Merit Planner might seem old-fashioned—but its simplicity, accessibility, and reliability are unmatched by any organizer—paper or electronic. It has ample space for weekends and evenings, so you can more realistically plan out every moment of your day. There's no learning curve. And since it's on paper, it will never crash and it will always be immediately available on the top of your desk. At the same time, it's small enough to take wherever you go.

Need Help? Call 831.462.5655

How to Get Started?

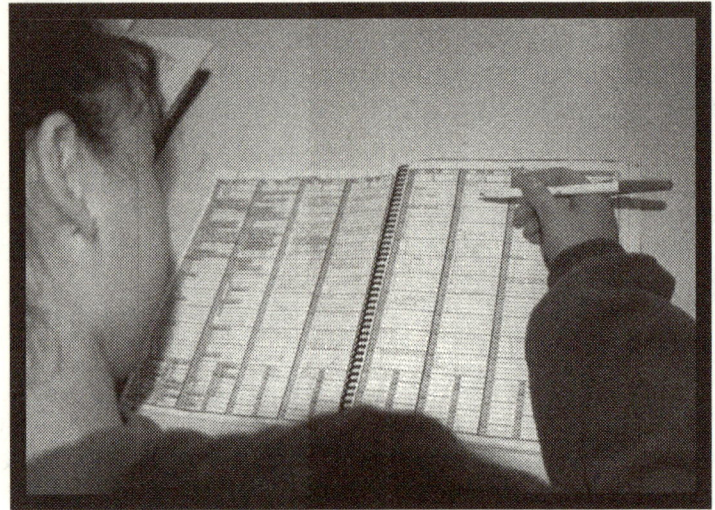

Block off time in your planner to complete each task.

Chapter II

Start Entering Tasks in Your Planner!

I recommend entering different types of tasks into the planner in a specific order. Don't just randomly start adding things in. We will start with the tasks whose times are fixed, such as appointments and meetings, working on to the tasks whose times are most flexible, such as errands and recreation. Then we will enter deadlines for long-term projects. Next, we will work backwards, entering in all the subtasks that must be done to complete these projects. The timeslots that are left over are perfect for scheduling odd chores and errands. Finally, you can reward yourself by scheduling in time just for you! In this chapter, I will guide you through this process, focusing in on the short-term tasks. The following chapter focuses more on long-term goals that require you to do many subtasks.

Keep a Journal of your Time

Before you get going, it helps to use the planner as a journal of how you're currently spending your day.

Need Help? Call 831.462.5655

Start Entering Tasks in Your Planner!

This will give you a baseline to start planning from. Afterwards, you'll look back in amazement at how much time you've been squandering every day.

To keep the journal of your time, carry your planner with you for a couple typical days and write in it everything you're doing during the day—from the time you wake up until the time you go to sleep. Don't overlook the seemingly insignificant things either. Often times, little things that we don't remember have a way of eating away at our time. We might think that lunch only takes a few minutes, but once you count in preparation, cooking, eating, and cleanup, you'll be shocked to find it actually takes well over an hour. Driving time has a way of adding up, even quick little errands. Some people don't realize that they spend countless hours gossiping on the phone or playing online solitaire. If you do something like this, re-evaluate whether you should really be devoting so much time to it.

Once you have a realistic picture of how your time is actually being spent, you can more realistically decide how much time to allot to each task. It's easy to get overly optimistic and plan to do more than you are really able to do in a given amount of time.

Make a List of all your Tasks

By now, your memory should be jogged and you should have a good picture of everything you regularly do. But before you move onto scheduling further into the future, make a complete list. Look at the journal of your time and your old planners and calendars. Then quiz your memory. Don't forget anything. Consider what tasks occur routinely in your life. What do you do on a daily, weekly, and monthly basis? Each day, you will at least be setting a time for waking up, going to sleep, eating your meals, and going to work, but what else is there? Do you have classes or do laundry on a weekly basis? What things do you do once a year?

Need Help? Visit www.meritworld.com

Today's Tasks

Now consider what appointments you have made. Rank each tasks according to how flexible or inflexible its time is. Once you have a prioritized list, you can write it into the schedule.

Today's Tasks

Let's start entering in today's tasks. Give yourself an uninterrupted hour or two to get this done. Find today's date in your planner (paperclip the upper left corner to make it easy to find the current date every time you open the book). Start by entering the time you got up this morning. If you got up before 9:00 am, like most working people, enter the time on the first line in the column. Enter "leave" next to the time you left the house.

Now continue to list all of the tasks that you've done so far today in their time slots. If you worked on certain tasks, such as making phone calls for one hour, enter "calls" and draw a line down to the time that you completed the last phone call. Tasks that are quick and easy can be bunched together and named "organize office" or "go online." When you've entered everything up to now, go ahead and enter " planner" and draw a line down to the time that you'll finish this task.

Next, enter the things that you will need to do for the rest of the day. Since your day doesn't end at 5:00 p.m., go ahead and enter everything else you plan to do in the evening. Block off time for preparing dinner, helping with homework, and doing the laundry. Remember those special shows that you can't miss, and plan your evening around them if you must. If you plan ahead, you'll see that you'll be able to get your work done and watch you're your favorite show too.

The Rest of the Week's Tasks

Now that you have the hang of entering tasks into your daily planner, go ahead and fill in all tasks for

Need Help? Call 831.462.5655

Start Entering Tasks in Your Planner!

the rest of the week. Transfer tasks off of the prioritized list into the schedule itself, starting with the least flexible tasks. It's also important to enter in recurring tasks each day, even routine ones. That way you can plan around them.

Fill in the Rest of the Month/Year's Tasks

Although this may seem like overkill, enter as much of your schedule as you can predict for the rest of the year. Unless your regular schedule is unpredictable or changes drastically, it's in your best interest to have an entire year ahead laid out for you. If you get asked if you're available on a certain date in the future, you'll be able to look at it and see your entire schedule. You'll have the foresight to make smart choices about adding new obligations to your already very busy schedule.

Think about all the tasks you have to take care of on a less frequent basis. Don't forget to enter the meeting with your accountant for your annual tax returns. Enter dates when you should meet, and then set a date to gather information you'll need for the meeting. Since you're really on a roll now, go ahead and enter dates of annual medical and dental checkups for you and your family. Even though you may not need to book the actual appointment that far in advance, enter "call for dental appointment" as a task on a weekday when you may have a few extra minutes to book appointments.

Don't Forget Important Dates

Rack your brain to remember all of those important dates. Think about important holidays and the birthdays of friends, family, and co-workers. Add important dates like anniversaries and holidays. If you've purchased tickets to a baseball game, enter the date in so that you don't schedule over it. Also add in theater nights, playoff games for your kids, the Scouts honor awards night, dance recitals, and whatever other family events.

Need Help? Visit www.meritworld.com

Sample Planner Page: Today's Tasks

Mon., Dec. 13		Tue., Dec. 14		Wed., Dec. 15	
7:00	Exercise	7:00		7:00	
7:30	Shower	7:30		7:30	
8:00	Leave for Day Care	8:00		8:00	
8:30	Drop off Jaclyn	8:30		8:30	
9:00	Calls	9:00		9:00	
9:15		9:15		9:15	
9:30		9:30		9:30	
9:45		9:45		9:45	
10:00		10:00		10:00	
10:15		10:15		10:15	
10:30	Meet with Rob	10:30		10:30	
10:45		10:45		10:45	
11:00		11:00		11:00	
11:15		11:15		11:15	
11:30	Finish Budget	11:30		11:30	
11:45	Report	11:45		11:45	
12:00	(Drive)	12:00		12:00	
12:15	lunch w/ Gail	12:15		12:15	
12:30	at Cafe Cruz	12:30		12:30	
12:45	* take Ross' gift	12:45		12:45	
1:00	(Drive)	1:00		1:00	
1:15		1:15		1:15	
1:30	Check Email	1:30		1:30	
1:45		1:45		1:45	
2:00		2:00		2:00	
2:15	Write New Proposal	2:15		2:15	
2:30		2:30		2:30	
2:45		2:45		2:45	
3:00		3:00		3:00	
3:15		3:15		3:15	
3:30		3:30		3:30	
3:45	Board Meeting	3:45		3:45	
4:00		4:00		4:00	
4:15		4:15		4:15	
4:30		4:30		4:30	
4:45		4:45		4:45	
5:00		5:00		5:00	
5:15	(Drive)	5:15		5:15	
5:30	Pick up Jaclyn	5:30		5:30	
5:45	Grocery Shopping	5:45		5:45	
6:00	Cookies for Thur	6:00		6:00	
6:15		6:15		6:15	
6:30	(Drive)	6:30		6:30	
6:45	Dinner: BBQ	6:45		6:45	
7:00	Chicken 9:30	7:00	9:30	7:00	9:30
7:15	Rice, Sal 9:45	7:15	9:45	7:15	9:45
7:30	Dishes 10:00 ER	7:30	10:00	7:30	10:00
7:45	Bath JD 10:15	7:45	10:15	7:45	10:15
8:00	Story 10:30	8:00	10:30	8:00	10:30
8:15	10:45	8:15	10:45	8:15	10:45
8:30	Laundry 11:00 News	8:30	11:00	8:30	11:00
8:45	Lunches 11:15	8:45	11:15	8:45	11:15
9:00	11:30 Bed	9:00	11:30	9:00	11:30
9:15	Laundry 11:45	9:15	11:45	9:15	11:45

Need Help? Call 831.462.5655

Start Entering Tasks in Your Planner!

Keep it Realistic

Write down everything you can imagine so you don't have to be burdened with remembering. Calling business associates for lunch, getting your hair colored, or meeting with your investment broker are all tasks that, if you don't plan for them, will slip by. Simply write "Call John Palmer for lunch date" in your planner to remind you.

Schedule for the Holidays

When planning the rest of the year, make sure to consider in the holiday season. Many of us ignore it, then get stuck running around and buying gifts at the last minute. You can avoid the rush if you plan out all your holiday shopping and your special affairs ahead of time. Schedule time for sending out greeting cards and getting family photographs, as well as special time to be with your family.

Keep it Realistic

Make sure that you're keeping your schedule realistic. If you aren't, then you're only going to cause problems, and soon you'll find it hard to stick with the program. Keep in mind that it may take a few weeks for you to fine-tune your schedule to a realistic load, so don't get too frustrated with problems when you first get started. But do look out for situations where your schedule is getting unrealistic. There are two things to especially be alert for:

First, we tend to underestimate the amount of times that activities will take. Do you schedule yourself fifteen minutes for a commute that sometimes takes fifteen minutes but often takes longer, or do you give yourself an hour to write a letter, when it often takes you several drafts? Allow yourself more time. Don't set yourself up for situations where you are forced to rush, because rushing can cause its own problems, such as traffic accidents and grammatical errors. If you consistently underestimate, it will throw the rest of your

Need Help? Call 831.462.5655

Start Entering Tasks in Your Planner!

day behind schedule and you will find yourself playing catch-up. Allot yourself enough time, and seek extra help when necessary.

Second, we tend to overestimate the number of things we can get done in one day. When we look at a schedule, it's easy to pack the days from morning to night with activity after activity, while not thinking about how completely exhausted you'll feel by the evening. After all, it's easy to assume you'll feel exactly as rested and alert as you are when you're setting the schedule. Make sure to schedule yourself enough time to breathe every day.

Sample Planner Page: Week-Long Schedule

Fri., Dec. 20	Sat., Dec. 21	Sun., Dec. 22
7:00 Exercise	7:00 Exercise	7:00 Exercise
7:30 Shower	7:30 Shower	7:30 Shower
8:00 Leave for Day Care	8:00 Leave for Day Care	8:00 Leave for Day Care
8:30 Drop off Jaclyn	8:30 Drop off Jaclyn	8:30 Drop off Jaclyn
9:00 Calls	9:00 Calls	9:00 Calls
9:15	9:15	9:15
9:30	9:30	9:30
9:45	9:45	9:45
10:00	10:00	10:00
10:15	10:15	10:15
10:30 Meet with Rob	10:30 Review Grant	10:30 Write Training Prog
10:45	10:45	10:45
11:00	11:00	11:00
11:15	11:15	11:15
11:30 Finish Budget Report	11:30 Finish Cover Letter	11:30 Email Headqtrs Review
11:45 (Drive)	11:45 (Drive)	11:45 Check Email
12:00 Lunch w/ Gail	12:00 Errands:	12:00 Lunch at office
12:15 at Cafe Cruz	12:15 Longs: Meds, Card	12:15 Check for Xmas flights
12:30 * take Ross' gift	12:30 Cleaners: 5 items	12:30
12:45	12:45 Blockbuster: Ret 3	12:45
1:00 (Drive)	1:00 (Drive)	1:00 Layout new brochure
1:15 Check Email	1:15 Check Email	1:15
1:30	1:30	1:30
1:45	1:45	1:45
2:00 Write New Proposal	2:00 Conference Call: Sam	2:00 Dr. Whitaker
2:15	2:15 1. Finalize dates	2:15 1. Eval Meds
2:30	2:30 2. Budget Approval	2:30 2. Rev Test Results
2:45	2:45 3. Recom Computer	2:45 3. Pain in Rt Arm
3:00	3:00 Interviews (3)	3:00
3:15	3:15	3:15 Finish Training Prog
3:30 Board Meeting	3:30	3:30
3:45	3:45	3:45
4:00	4:00	4:00
4:15	4:15	4:15
4:30	4:30 Email Thorin	4:30
4:45	4:45 Backup System	4:45 Email Ind Contr forms
5:00 (Drive)	5:00 (Drive)	5:00
5:15 Pick up Jaclyn	5:15 Pick up Jaclyn	5:15 Pick up Jaclyn
5:30 Grocery Shopping	5:30 (Drive)	5:30
5:45 Cookies for Thur	5:45 Dinner: Chinese Salad	5:45 Dinner: Taco Salad
6:00	6:00	6:00
6:15 (Drive)	6:15 Dishes	6:15 Dishes
6:30 Dinner: BBQ Chicken	6:30	6:30 Laundry
6:45 Rice, Salad	6:45	6:45
7:00 Dishes 9:30	7:00 9:30	7:00 9:30
7:15 Bath JD 9:45	7:15 9:45	7:15 9:45
7:30 Story 10:00 Fav Show	7:30 Bath JD 10:00 Fav Show	7:30 Bath JD 10:00 News
7:45 10:15	7:45 Story 10:15	7:45 Story 10:15
8:00 Laundry 10:30	8:00 Lunches 10:30	8:00 Lunches 10:30
8:15 Lunches 10:45	8:15 10:45	8:15 Laundry 10:45
8:30 11:00 News	8:30 11:00 News	8:30 11:00 Time Mag
8:45 Laundry 11:15	8:45 11:15	8:45 11:15
9:00 11:30 Bed	9:00 11:30 Bed	9:00 11:30 Bed
9:15 11:45	9:15 11:45	9:15 11:45

Need Help? Call 831.462.5655

Start Entering Tasks in Your Planner!

Chapter III

Planning Ahead for Long-Term Goals

We all have had big dreams, but too often those dreams elude us because we can never seem to follow through. Whether you want to write a book, remodel the house, or go back to school—these goals often just seem daunting. But believe me, it can be done. After all, I managed to write and publish this book and three others. And I did it by following this program. To meet your long-term goals, you're going to need to take a more detailed approach. In this chapter, I will show you how to manage your time to make your long-term goals a reality.

Start with a List

Now that your routine schedule is laid out in your planner, draw up a list of long-term goals and important due dates. There are some things you're required to do, but also ask yourself *what else is it that I really want to accomplish?* Make a list of these things.

Need Help? Call 831.462.5655

Planning Ahead for Long-Term Goals

You might start with career-related tasks. Enter dates that reports are due as well as dates to prepare mailings or to design new programs or proposals. Go ahead and enter deadlines for career decisions so that you have ample time to act upon them. Stop and think about ongoing projects. Write down the date that you aim to complete the project.

Next, think about what you'd personally like to accomplish. Do you want to start your own business? Do you want to plan a vacation abroad? Do you want to find a better job? Add these to your list. Don't worry about how overwhelming they might seem. If you write down date to accomplish these things, then you have a more tangible deadline to motivate you. You can do it!

Break up the Subtasks

Now that you know when you need to complete your projects, it's time to break the larger projects into subtasks. Breaking projects up makes them less overwhelming and more manageable. No longer will it appear that you have to conquer an insurmountable project—but instead it will look like a series of very reasonable little tasks. When planning, most people fail to break up projects like this, which causes them to misestimate how much time a project really takes. Not surprisingly, they either cave in to their apprehensions, or they will find themselves stuck in an 11th-hour crisis. That's why this step is so important.

Again, it's easiest to start with a list that you will later transfer into your planner. Next to each long-term goal, list all the subtasks it requires. Estimate how much time each subtask demands, and write that amount next to each. It's smart to overestimate the amount of time in order to be safe if things happen to run behind schedule.

Need Help? Visit www.meritworld.com

Project Plan

Project Plan		
Download grant off internet	- 45 min.	- 1 day
Preview other grant proposals	- 3 hours	- 2 days
Read grant guidelines	- 30 min.	- 1 day
Write grant proposal (1st draft)	- 3 hours	- 2 days
Do research for grant	- 4 to 6 hours	- 3 days
Distribute grant to editors	- 6 days	- 6 days
Make final edits to grant	- 3 hours	- 1 day
Make copies of grant	- 1 hour	- 1 day
Review instructions and package grant for mailing	- 2 hours	- 1 day
Go to post office to mail grant	- 1 hour	- 1 day
Total days to complete project		- 19 days
Add 3 days (unforeseen problems)		- 3 days
Total days to complete project		- 22 days

1. Enter the deadline date in your planner (3 days earlier than the posted date).

2. Then enter tasks in your planner by starting at the bottom of the Project Plan and work your way back from the deadline.

April

Sunday	Monday	Tuesday	Wednesday	Thursday	Friday	Saturday
					Download Grant (Day 1) — 1	2
3	Preview Other Prop (Day 2) — 4	5	Read Guidelines (Day 4) — 6	Write Proposal (Day 5) — 7	8	9
10	Final Research (Day 7) — 11	12	13	Editors Rev Proj (Day 10) — 14	15	16
17	18	19	Receive Comments (Day 14) — 20	Final Edits (Day 15) — 21	Copy Grant (Day 16) — 22	23
24	Rev Instr Prep Mail (Day 17) — 25	Post Office (Day 18) — 26	Project Deadline (Day 19) — 27	28	29	Real Project Deadline — 30

Need Help? Call 831.462.5655

Planning Ahead for Long-Term Goals

Enter the Times into the Planner

Now that you have a list of the deadlines for your long-term goals and a list of all the required subtasks, enter them into the planner. Start by entering the deadline. Then enter the subtasks. Work backwards, starting with the subtask, which must be done last and work your way to the one that must be done first. If your work has tight deadlines, plan accordingly. It's smart to plan to have everything done a couple days in advance. That way, you're covered in case things run behind schedule. If you find that you've given yourself too much or too little time for all the subtasks, then you might need to adjust the final deadline accordingly.

My Success Story

I used this process of long-term planning to write a grant proposal for a school project. I entered the deadline in my planner. Then on scratch paper, I listed all of the subtasks: download the grant off of the internet, preview other grant proposals, write the grant proposal, do research, distribute the proposal for editing, read the edited grant proposal, make copies, package up the grant proposal, and go to the post office.

Once I had listed all of the subtasks, I entered how much time each subtask would take, and how long I expected it would take to receive responses from others. Finally, I added up the time to determine how long the entire project would take, and then I worked backwards from my due date to determine when I should actually start working on the project. I planned to complete everything three days early, just in case it ran behind schedule. Then I pulled out my planner and scheduled each subtask into my schedule. Because I already had my complete schedule in my planner, I knew what other commitments I would need to plan around. I managed to complete the grant on time without any major delays, and I ended up receiving the grant!

Need Help? Visit www.meritworld.com

Sample Planner Page: Notes Section

Sat.,		Sun.,		Reminders/Notes
7:00		7:00		
7:30		7:30		Jaclyn's B-day Party
8:00		8:00		Guest List:
8:30		8:30		Ariel
9:00		9:00		Ethan
9:15		9:15		Jessie
9:30		9:30		Schyler
9:45		9:45		Trevor
10:00		10:00		Darcy
10:15		10:15		Nicole
10:30		10:30		Ross
10:45		10:45		Kaitlin
11:00		11:00		Lauryn
11:15		11:15		
11:30		11:30		Party Theme:
11:45		11:45		~~Hawaiian~~
12:00		12:00		Pirates of the Caribbean
12:15		12:15		~~50s~~
12:30		12:30		~~Cats~~
12:45		12:45		
1:00		1:00		Party Foods
1:15		1:15		Hot dogs
1:30		1:30		Hot dog buns
1:45		1:45		Ketchup
2:00		2:00		Mustard
2:15		2:15		Relish
2:30		2:30		Chips
2:45		2:45		Lemonade
3:00		3:00		Chocolate cake
3:15		3:15		Chocolate ice cream
3:30		3:30		Pretzels
3:45		3:45		Assorted crackers
4:00		4:00		
4:15		4:15		Game and Activities
4:30		4:30		Pin the Tail on Pirate
4:45		4:45		Make a Pirates Hat
5:00		5:00		Dress up like Pirates
5:15		5:15		
5:30		5:30		Accessories
5:45		5:45		Plates, cups, utensils
6:00		6:00		Balloons
6:15		6:15		Tablecloth/napkins
6:30		6:30		Prizes
6:45		6:45		Games
7:00	9:30	7:00	9:30	Invitations
7:15	9:45	7:15	9:45	Candles
7:30	10:00	7:30	10:00	
7:45	10:15	7:45	10:15	
8:00	10:30	8:00	10:30	
8:15	10:45	8:15	10:45	
8:30	11:00	8:30	11:00	
8:45	11:15	8:45	11:15	
9:00	11:30	9:00	11:30	**Family Meeting**
9:15	11:45	9:15	11:45	

Need Help? Call 831.462.5655

Planning Ahead for Long-Term Goals

My Success Story

Do this type of planning for all of your large projects—even your children's school projects. Just so you don't go nuts when your child walks into your bedroom at 9:00 p.m. in tears telling you about a project that is due tomorrow, set aside time to help your children organize their projects. Block off time to brainstorm about the project, buy the materials, build it, and polish it up. Reports, both yours and your children's, need vast amounts of time to be completed. Think about all the subtasks: choosing a topic, finding the resources at the local libraries and on the internet, reading the information, taking notes, writing the outline, writing the rough draft, editing the draft, letting the project rest, doing the final editing, adding pictures and tables, adding the table of contents, bibliography, index, appendices. Each step needs to be completed on time in order to stay on schedule.

When blocking off time for the subtasks in your planner, make sure that your personal and other work responsibilities are blocked off so you are scheduling realistic time to get each task done.

Do you have projects that don't have deadlines? Place these odd projects in your notes sections on the far right column of the weeks that you think you might have time to get them done. As soon as you find a time slot during that week to do the task, enter it in your daily schedule and cross it off the list in the notes section. Because lists tend to be daunting, it's best to move them from the Notes section and into your regular schedule as soon as possible.

Need Help? Call 831.462.5655

Planning Ahead for Long-Term Goals

Chapter IV
Living by the Planner

It's not enough to just be entering your entire schedule in the planner. All this preparation will be squandered if you aren't actually using the planner on a day-to-day basis. This chapter will show you how to effectively make use of the planner throughout the day and how to adapt to all the scheduling obstacles that get thrown at you.

Consult the Planner Often

Since you use the planner to plan your entire day, you should check it often. Check your planner when you wake up in the morning and several times throughout the day. If your schedule is very intricate, make sure to check it even more often.

Have the Planner Nearby

When you're at home or at work, keep it on top of your desk. That way, you can always access it easily without having to dig through clutter. Keep the planner

Need Help? Call 831.462.5655

Living by the Planner

open to the current day. You don't want to waste your time constantly flipping around.

When you leave the house, take the planner (and a pencil) with you. If you keep the planner with you all throughout the day, then you will always be prepared. Any task that pops into your mind when you're out can quickly get entered into the planner before you forget.

Just the other day, I was at the supermarket when I remembered that my daughter needed me to pick up some supplies for her science project. I didn't have time to do it that day, but since I had my planner with me, I was able to schedule in that errand for later that week. If I hadn't, I could just imagine how upset she would have been when I forgot to bring her supplies.

Readjusting to Changes

Only in a perfect world will things run according to the schedule like clockwork, which is why you have been filling it in using pencil. Be flexible at regrouping when plans change, so you can still stay in control. When things happen that change your schedule, simply erase the tasks and reschedule them for a future block of time. If you realize that a deadline will not be met, be proactive and contact the relevant people to see about rescheduling.

Highlight off Completed Tasks

Throughout the day, highlight whatever tasks have been completed to indicate that they are out of the way and out of mind. Highlighting not only brings a sense of relief, but also a sense of satisfaction, because you have a written record of all you have accomplished in the day. Think of the highlighting as a little reward.

Sample Planner Page: Transferring Tasks

Mon., Jan. 3		Tue., Jan. 4			Wed., Jan. 5		
7:00 Exercise		7:00 Exercise			7:00 Exercise		
7:30 Shower		7:30 Shower			7:30 Shower		
8:00 Leave for Day Care		8:00 Leave for Day Care			8:00 Leave for Day Care		
8:30 Drop off Jaclyn		8:30 Drop off Jaclyn			8:30 Drop off Jaclyn		
9:00 Calls		9:00 Calls			9:00 Calls		
9:15		9:15			9:15		
9:30		9:30			9:30		
9:45		9:45			9:45		
10:00		10:00			10:00		
10:15		10:15			10:15		
10:30 Meet with Rob		10:30 Review Grant			10:30 Write Training Prog		
10:45		10:45			10:45		
11:00		11:00			11:00		
11:15		11:15			11:15		
11:30 Finish Budget Report		11:30 Finish Cover Letter			11:30 Email Headqtrs Review		
11:45 (Drive)		11:45 (Drive)			11:45 Check Email		
12:00 Lunch w/ Gail		12:00 ~~Errands: Flat Tire AAA~~			12:00 Lunch at office		
12:15 at Cafe Cruz		12:15 ~~Longs: Meds, Card~~			12:15 Check for Xmas flights		
12:30 * take Ross' gift		12:30 ~~Cleaners: 5 items~~			12:30		
12:45		12:45 ~~Blockbuster: Ret 3~~			12:45		
1:00 (Drive)		1:00 (Drive)			1:00 Layout new brochure		
1:15 Check Email		1:15 Check Email			1:15		
1:30		1:30			1:30		
1:45		1:45			1:45		
2:00 Write New Proposal		2:00 Conference Call: Sam			2:00 Dr. Whitaker		
2:15		2:15 1. Finalize dates			2:15 1. Eval Meds		
2:30		2:30 2. Budget Approval			2:30 2. Rev Test Results		
2:45		2:45 3. Recom. Computer			2:45 3. Pain in Rt Arm		
3:00		3:00 (interviews (3)			3:00		
3:15		3:15			3:15 Finish Training Prog		
3:30 Board Meeting		3:30			3:30		
3:45		3:45			3:45		
4:00		4:00			4:00		
4:15		4:15			4:15		
4:30		4:30 Email Thorin			4:30		
4:45		4:45 Backup System			4:45 Email Ind Contr forms		
5:00 (Drive)		5:00 (Drive)			5:00		
5:15 Pick up Jaclyn		5:15 Pick up Jaclyn			5:15 Pick up Jaclyn		
5:30 Grocery Shopping		5:30 (Drive)			5:30 Errands:		
5:45 Cookies for Thur		5:45 Dinner: Chinese Salad			5:45 Longs: Meds, Card		
6:00		6:00			6:00 Cleaners: 5 items		
6:15 (Drive)		6:15 Dishes			6:15 Blockbuster: Ret 3		
6:30 Dinner: BBQ Chicken		6:30			6:30 Dinner: Fast Food		
6:45 Rice, Salad		6:45			6:45		
7:00 Dishes	9:30	7:00	9:30		7:00 Laundry	9:30	
7:15 Bath JD	9:45	7:15	9:45		7:15	9:45	
7:30 Story	10:00	7:30 Bath JD	10:00 ER		7:30 Bath JD	10:00 News	
7:45	10:15	7:45 Story	10:15		7:45 Story	10:15	
8:00 Laundry	10:30	8:00 Lunches	10:30		8:00 Lunches	10:30	
8:15 Lunches	10:45	8:15	10:45		8:15 Laundry	10:45	
8:30	11:00	8:30	11:00 News		8:30	11:00 Time Mag	
8:45 Laundry	11:15	8:45	11:15		8:45	11:15	
9:00	11:30	9:00	11:30 Bed		9:00	11:30 Bed	
9:15	11:45	9:15	11:45		9:15	11:45	

Need Help? Call 831.462.5655

Living by the Planner

Sample Planner Page: Highlighted Day

Mon., Jan. 3	Tue., Jan. 4	Wed., Jan. 5
7:00 Exercise	7:00 Exercise	7:00 Exercise
7:30 Shower	7:30 Shower	7:30 Shower
8:00 Leave for Day Care	8:00 Leave for Day Care	8:00 Leave for Day Care
8:30 Drop off Jaclyn	8:30 Drop off Jaclyn	8:30 Drop off Jaclyn
9:00 Calls	9:00 Calls	9:00 Calls
9:15	9:15	9:15
9:30	9:30	9:30
9:45	9:45	9:45
10:00	10:00	10:00
10:15	10:15	10:15
10:30 Meet with Rob	10:30 Review Grant	10:30 Write Training Prog
10:45	10:45	10:45
11:00	11:00	11:00
11:15	11:15	11:15
11:30 Finish Budget Report	11:30 Finish Cover Letter	11:30 Email Headqtrs Review
11:45 (Drive)	11:45 (Drive)	11:45 Check Email
12:00 Lunch w/ Gail	12:00 Errands: Flat Tire AAA	12:00 Lunch at office
12:15 at Cafe Cruz	12:15 Longs: Meds, Card	12:15 Check for Xmas flights
12:30 * take Ross' gift	12:30 Cleaners: 5 items	12:30
12:45	12:45 Blockbuster: Ret 3	12:45
1:00 (Drive)	1:00 (Drive)	1:00 Layout new brochure
1:15 Check Email	1:15 Check Email	1:15
1:30	1:30	1:30
1:45	1:45	1:45
2:00 Write New Proposal	2:00 Conference Call: Sam	2:00 Dr. Whitaker
2:15	2:15 1. Finalize dates	2:15 1. Eval Meds
2:30	2:30 2. Budget Approval	2:30 2. Rev Test Results
2:45	2:45 3. Recom Computer	2:45 3. Pain in Rt Arm
3:00	3:00 Interviews (3)	3:00
3:15	3:15	3:15 Finish Training Prog
3:30 Board Meeting	3:30	3:30
3:45	3:45	3:45
4:00	4:00	4:00
4:15	4:15	4:15
4:30	4:30 Email Thorin	4:30
4:45	4:45 Backup System	4:45 Email Ind Contr forms
5:00 (Drive)	5:00 (Drive)	5:00
5:15 Pick up Jaclyn	5:15 Pick up Jaclyn	5:15 Pick up Jaclyn
5:30	5:30 (Drive)	5:30 Errands:
5:45 Grocery Shopping	5:45 Dinner: Chinese Salad	5:45 Longs: Meds, Card
6:00 Cookies for Thur	6:00	6:00 Cleaners: 5 items
6:15 (Drive)	6:15 Dishes	6:15 Blockbuster: Ret 3
6:30 Dinner: BBQ Chicken	6:30	6:30 Dinner: Fast Food
6:45 Rice, salad	6:45	6:45
7:00 Dishes 9:30	7:00 9:30	7:00 Laundry 9:30
7:15 Bath JD 9:45	7:15 9:45	7:15 9:45
7:30 Story 10:00 TV	7:30 Bath JD 10:00 ER	7:30 Bath JD 10:00 News
7:45 10:15	7:45 Story 10:15	7:45 Story 10:15
8:00 Laundry 10:30	8:00 Lunches 10:30	8:00 Lunches 10:30
8:15 Lunches 10:45	8:15 10:45	8:15 Laundry 10:45
8:30 11:00 News	8:30 11:00 News	8:30 11:00 Time Mag
8:45 Laundry 11:15	8:45 11:15	8:45 11:15
9:00 11:30 Bed	9:00 11:30 Bed	9:00 11:30 Bed
9:15 11:45	9:15 11:45	9:15 11:45

Need Help? Call 831.462.5655

Living by the Planner

After-the-Fact Entries

In order to keep your planner realistic, enter tasks and projects that you have done, even though you hadn't scheduled them. Then highlight them off. That way, when you look back, you have a permanent record to fully account for your time. Not only will you feel more accomplished, but you also retain proof that the task was done.

Didn't do the Task, Now What?

What if by the end of the day you didn't complete everything you had planned? Don't leave these tasks unresolved. You might forget about them. Tasks that haven't gotten done by the end of the day will need to be rescheduled into the future. By moving the task forward, it takes the pressure and guilt off of you for not completing the job at the original time. At the end of the day, put a big cross through the day to indicate that you're done and that you're ready for tomorrow. You don't want to start a new day with the burden of having to dig through the past for incomplete tasks.

If you reschedule a task to another day, don't forget to inform those who may be affected by the change. Schedule a time to contact them. This courtesy, if given with plenty of notice, is usually well received by the recipient.

Lapses in Use

If you go a day where you neglected to use your planner, don't let it become a habit. Maybe it just slipped your mind when you got carried away with a lengthy phone call, or maybe you rushed out of the house and left the planner there all day. After all your hard work and resolution, don't let yourself cave in. Just go back to the planner as soon as you get the chance and see what you'll need to do to get caught up. Look back through the times when you weren't using it, and look

Need Help? Call 831.462.5655

Living by the Planner

at each of the tasks that you haven't highlighted off. Hopefully, you did most of them even though you didn't have the planner. But the ones that are incomplete will need to be rescheduled into the future.

If the lapses in use become more frequent, think about why it keeps happening. There are several possibilities. It might be that you are setting a schedule that's too unrealistic to follow. It might be that you don't have enough motivation. Or it could be something else. Once you figure out why you're lapsing, take appropriate action to address the problem. If you need more help with motivation, see the chapter titled *A Word on Motivation*.

Chapter V

Keeping Track of your Family and their Schedules

Even if you've transformed yourself into a model of organization, you'll still be running late and missing appointments if your family is not just as organized. You interact with your family throughout the day and you participate in many of the same activities, so when they mismanage their time, it spills over into your schedule. That's why the next step is to coordinate your schedule with the schedules of your other family members.

Add in Kids' Schedules

The important thing is to have your kids' schedules centralized in your planner. If you have a family calendar on your refrigerator at home, that's not going to help you when you're at the office. All that information needs to be in your planner. Write your kids' regular schedule on one of the notes pages in the back of your planner. Then write the rest of their schedule—including times, locations, and activities—on the month page in your planner. This gives you a chance to view it at a glance. If

Keeping Track of your Family and their Schedules

you're really meticulous, you can even add your children's schedules on the far right side of your daily columns, which makes them more convenient for you to see.

Transportation for the Kids

Having the kids' schedule is especially important if you plan their transportation or coordinate their carpool. No mother wants to think about their child alone and stranded after practice. But with everything you have to do, it's easy for your responsibility slip your mind.

Carpooling is a smart idea for busy mothers. Not only does it save lots of driving time for all the families, but it also reduces both the money we spend on gas and the congestion we create on the roads. If you are driving your child everywhere they have to go, talk to other parents to see about setting up a carpool. Or you might look into having your child walk, ride a bike, or use public transportation. All of these solutions give you more time to do things more productive than sitting behind the wheel.

If you carpool or share driving responsibilities with your spouse, place the initials of the driver next to each activity. If there is a different driver to and from an activity, then make sure to note them both. If you are scheduled to drive, then enter it in your daily section of your planner. In order to avoid miscues, regularly confirm with other drivers who is scheduled to drive when and where.

By having the children's schedules in your planner, you'll know where your child is throughout the day. If there's an emergency, you know who to call. And you will also know who to contact if your child becomes ill and needs to cancel, or even if you just want to make a motherly call to check up that everyone got where they needed.

Need Help? Visit www.meritworld.com

Carpool Schedule

Carpool Schedule

April

Sunday	Monday	Tuesday	Wednesday	Thursday	Friday	Saturday
					1 RD: JD only	2
3	4 SD: JD, AB, ND, IC	5 CB: JD, AB, ND, IC	6 RD: JD, AB, ND, IC	7 GJ: JD, AB, ND, IC	8 RD: JD, ND	9
10	11 SD: JD, AB, ND, IC	12 CB: JD, AB, ND, IC	13 RD: JD, AB, ND, IC	14 GJ: JD, AB, ND, IC	15 RD: JD, ND	16
17	18 SD: JD, AB, ND, IC	19 SD: JD, AB, ND, IC	20 SD: JD, AB, ND, IC	21 SD: JD, AB, ND, IC	22 SD: JD, ND	23
24	25 SD: JD, AB, ND, IC	26 CB: JD, AB, ND, IC	27 RD: JD, AB, ND, IC	28 GJ: JD, AB, ND, IC	29 RD: JD, ND	30

Need Help? Call 831.462.5655

Keeping Track of your Family and their Schedules

Carpool Schedule in Planner

Mon., Jan. 17 Martin Luther King Day		Tue., Jan. 18		Wed., Jan. 19	
7:00 Exercise		7:00 Exercise		7:00 Exercise	
7:30 Shower		7:30 Shower		7:30 Shower	
8:00 Leave for Day Care		8:00 Leave work JD w/ Gail		8:00 Leave work JD w/ Lori	
8:30 Drop off JD, AB, ND, IC		8:30 Calls		8:30 Calls	
9:00 Calls		9:00		9:00	
9:15		9:15		9:15	
9:30		9:30		9:30	
9:45		9:45		9:45	
10:00		10:00		10:00	
10:15		10:15		10:15	
10:30 Meet with Rob		10:30 Review Grant		10:30 Write Training Prog	
10:45		10:45		10:45	
11:00		11:00		11:00	
11:15		11:15		11:15	
11:30 Finish Budget Report		11:30 Finish Cover Letter		11:30 Email Headqtrs Review	
11:45 (Drive)		11:45 (Drive)		11:45 Check Email	
12:00 Lunch w/ Gail		12:00 Errands:		12:00 Lunch at office	
12:15 at Cafe Cruz		12:15 Longs: Meds, Card		12:15 Check for Xmas flights	
12:30 * take Ross' gift		12:30 Cleaners: 5 items		12:30	
12:45		12:45 Blockbuster: Ret 3		12:45	
1:00 (Drive)		1:00 (Drive)		1:00 Layout new brochure	
1:15 Check Email		1:15 Check Email		1:15	
1:30		1:30		1:30	
1:45		1:45		1:45	
2:00 Write New Proposal		2:00 Conference Call: Sam		2:00 Dr. Whitaker	
2:15		2:15 1. Finalize dates		2:15 1. Eval Meds	
2:30		2:30 2. Budget Approval		2:30 2. Rev Test Results	
2:45		2:45 3. Recom Computer		2:45 3. Pain in Rt Arm	
3:00		3:00 Interviews (3)		3:00	
3:15		3:15		3:15 Finish Training Prog	
3:30 Board Meeting		3:30		3:30	
3:45		3:45		3:45	
4:00		4:00		4:00	
4:15		4:15		4:15	
4:30		4:30 Email Thorin		4:30	
4:45		4:45 Backup System		4:45 Email Ind Contr forms	
5:00 (Drive)		5:00 (Drive)		5:00 (Drive)	
5:15 Pick up Jaclyn		5:15 Pick up Jaclyn		5:15 RD p/u JD	
5:30 Grocery Shopping		5:30 (Drive)		5:30	
5:45 Cookies for Thur		5:45 Dinner: Chinese Salad		5:45 Dinner: Taco Salad	
6:00		6:00		6:00	
6:15 (Drive)		6:15 Dishes		6:15 Dishes	
6:30 Dinner: BBQ Chicken,		6:30		6:30 Laundry	
6:45 Ring Salad		6:45		6:45	
7:00 Dishes	9:30	7:00	9:30	7:00	9:30
7:15 Bath JD	9:45	7:15	9:45	7:15	9:45
7:30 Story	10:00	7:30 Bath JD	10:00 ER	7:30 Bath JD	10:00 News
7:45	10:15	7:45 Story	10:15	7:45 Story	10:15
8:00 Laundry	10:30	8:00 Lunches	10:30	8:00 Lunches	10:30
8:15 Lunches	10:45	8:15	10:45	8:15 Laundry	10:45
8:30	11:00	8:30	11:00 News	8:30	11:00 Time Mag
8:45 Laundry	11:15	8:45	11:15	8:45	11:15
9:00	11:30	9:00	11:30 Bed	9:00	11:30 Bed
9:15	11:45	9:15	11:45	9:15	11:45

Need Help? Call 831.462.5655

Keeping Track of your Family and their Schedules

Need Help? Visit www.meritworld.com

Coordinating with your Spouse

Keeping track of your spouse's entire daily schedule might be unnecessary, especially if it's fairly regular, but it's certainly necessary to know when big things that affect everyone are happening, such as when they're going to be out of town. In fact, it's also important to know when your spouse plans to be especially busy, because you're probably the one who has to cover all of their regular responsibilities to the family. You'll be better prepared for your spouse's absences if you take the time to plan out all the extra jobs you'll have to take on while they're gone.

If you'll be picking up the extra driving, errands, and cooking during their absence, block off the needed time in your planner. With good notice, you can easily manage. Double up on preparing dinners, ask the kids to help with lunches and breakfasts, and get help from other parents who can give rides.

Even if your spouse is not going on a long trip, but they simply have a meeting that will keep them out until after the kids are in bed, knowing ahead of time can prevent hassles. This may be a good time to use that pizza coupon you've been saving. That saves time cooking and cleaning in the kitchen, and still leaves you enough time to get home to help out with their homework.

Another Party?

If any of your children are in primary school or preschool, they are probably invited to dozens of birthday parties, so plan accordingly. Lots of time will be dedicated to responding to invitations, buying and wrapping gifts, getting a special outfit ready, and getting your child to and from the party. But don't let your personal schedule get dictated by every party invitation your child receives. You and your children will need to determine whose parties they'll attend and whose they won't. To politely

Need Help? Call 831.462.5655

Keeping Track of your Family and their Schedules

excuse your child from attending parties, thank the family while saying that the party conflicts with prior arrangements.

Since preparing for parties involves a series of small subtasks, you can approach them the same way you would approach a project—by scheduling out each of the individual subtasks. For each party your child will attend, schedule in time to purchase gifts and cards, as well as time to wrap the gifts. Plan your shopping list so that you can pick up whatever you need. By adding these tasks to your regular shopping schedule, these parties will have minimal impact on your schedule, so you can enjoy yourself without the pre-party stress.

After-School Activities

Children today take on an ambitious load of after-school activities, including sports, dance, music, tutoring, and academic clubs. These activities are important to the development of the child, but you and your family will need to find the right balance to make sure that they also have enough time for homework, family, and their friends.

Before signing them up, there are a few time factors to consider. Consider how heavy their homework workload is. Younger children have less homework, but they also go to bed earlier. Make sure that you aren't over-scheduling your child in a way that leaves them completely exhausted at the end of the day. Remember to also consider yourself into the equation. You may need to pick the days that your child can participate in after-school activities based more on your own schedule than on what your child most wants.

Once you sign your child up, make sure to enter the activity into your planner. Decide who will drive and enter the details in your planner like you did for their regular schedule.

Need Help? Visit www.meritworld.com

Chapter VI

Time Management for the Family

Once you get comfortable and appreciate the benefits of having your planner, get your family started on the same program. When your entire family uses their time efficiently, not only does everyone's life run smoother, but the entire family operates the way it is supposed to—like one coordinated unit.

Hold a Family Meeting to Get them Started

Pick a date when all family members are available for three uninterrupted hours and have everyone plan to be there. This will be the first of many family meetings. On your first family meeting date, let the answering machine take all of your calls, turn off the TV, and meet around the kitchen table. Get a planner for each family member. Now you're going to teach your family everything you've learned about organizing your life.

Time Management for the Family

Start Them at as Young as Six Years Old!

Children as young as six years old can learn how to use a planner. By starting so early, you reach them before they fall into bad habits and you give them the tools to succeed in the future. It's best to let young children fill in the planner themselves so they have control, but if they slow down the family, you can start them off and then let them finish later.

Enter in Kids' Schedules

Start by showing your kids how to enter in their regular schedules. This will include their schedule of sleeping and waking, their classes at school, their after-school activities for the week, and any other regular commitments. Of course, schedule in time for meals and for transportation. This process will run similarly to the way that you entered your own schedule.

Family Activities

Once the kids' school and after-school activities are blocked off in their appointment books, ask them to add in family commitments. If the family goes to church on Sundays, they can add this in for the entire year. Don't forget family vacations, reunions, birthdays, and anniversaries. As soon as you confirm family outings, dinner/party plans, theater/sports outings, let all family members know.

What about Homework?

Since kids spend a lot of time doing homework, you'll need to teach them how to include it in their schedule. This skill is especially important for older children, since they tend to have more homework. After you show kids how to use their homework, they will gain the independence to schedule time for it on their own.

Kids Shouldn't Keep Lists of Homework!

Kids Shouldn't Keep Lists of Homework!

Students who just keep lists set themselves up for all sorts of problems. Looking at a long list of homework is overwhelming. They might only consider the homework important if it is due the next day. And with only a list, children underestimate the amount of time they'll need to complete the work—setting themselves up for last-minute emergencies.

Instead, they need to schedule time for each assignment into their planners. Not only does this scheduling keep the children realistic, but it gives them a detailed plan to following through on. By blocking off thirty minutes to read a chapter, fifteen minutes to study new spelling words, plus an hour to do math problems, they'll see exactly how much time they'll need to get the work done. They can also prioritize tasks to see whether they have time for other activities. Students who use this technique feel less stressed and are more likely to succeed in school.

Scheduling Homework into the Planner

Next, have your kids enter due dates on the date that homework or projects are due—not when they are assigned. Also include test dates, field trips, and school holidays. They should block off time to complete all of the assignments, one assignment at a time. In other words, they shouldn't write in "homework" and block that off. They need to write in the exact homework assignment they will do and block off the amount of time they think they'll need to complete the assignment. Students get overwhelmed when they know they have a lot of homework to do but don't know where to begin to tackle it. But this problem is avoided if you schedule in each individual assignment.

High priority assignments and assignments that are due sooner should be scheduled to be completed before lower priority assignments and assignments with

Time Management for the Family

more distant due dates. Schedule in a little more item than you think is necessary, just in case they run behind schedule.

Long-Term Projects for Kids

Like with yourself, your kids' long-term projects will require more intricate planning. Most of your kids' long term projects will be related to school, such as reports, presentations, and big tests. If there are multiple steps to completing the project, they will need to enter in all steps. Just listing the task to do is not good enough. Begin by listing out all the tasks. Then enter them in the planner in reverse chronological order, starting with the task that must be done right before the project is complete.

For instance, if they're preparing for a test, they need to read the chapter, take reading notes, make flash cards, and review class notes. Starting from the test date, they should enter in specific blocks of time to do each task. This will help them to understand exactly what it is they have to do so they don't forget any part of the assignment. If each part of the homework assignment is not blocked off, students may forget to do it. But when they see how much time they will need to invest in their projects, they are learning how to control their time.

Organize the Entire Year

Ask them to fill in their entire class schedule and all after-school activities until the end of the semester or year, depending on whether or not classes change at the end of the semester. In elementary and middle school, the schedule of classes remains fairly constant throughout the year. High school students' schedules can change more often, so they may prefer to enter in their current schedule and enter their new schedule as soon as they get their list of classes. These students should block off time to enter their next semester's classes at the end of the current semester. It's important

Need Help? Visit www.meritworld.com

Sample Planner Page: Test Study Schedule

Time	Mon., Jan. 31	Tue., Feb. 1	Wed., Feb. 2
7:00	Shower	Shower	Shower
7:30	Breakfast	Breakfast	Breakfast
8:00	Leave for School	Leave for School	Leave for School
8:30	Homeroom	Homeroom	Homeroom
9:00			
9:15	English	History	English
9:30	Finish reading ch 2	Review Sheet due	Write critique
9:45			
10:00			
10:15			
10:30			
10:45	Math	Spanish	Math
11:00	pp 35: 1-35 odds	Spanish poster due	pp 37: 1-20 evens
11:15			
11:30			
11:45			
12:00			
12:15	Lunch	Lunch	Lunch
12:30			
12:45			
1:00			
1:15	Science	Music	Science
1:30	Lab writeup due	turn in forms	Quiz on Ch 2
1:45			
2:00			
2:15			
2:30			
2:45	Dad pick up	Mom Picks up	Take bus
3:00	Piano lessons	Chores: trash cans in	Chores: Vacuum LR
3:15		His: flashcards	His: Read notes
3:30			Rev flashcards
3:45	Chores: trash out		Rev worksheet
4:00	History worksheet		Take practice quiz
4:15		Eng: Finish critique	Span: Quiz self
4:30		spell check	Write words 10X
4:45			Rev flashcards
5:00	Spanish Poster:		Call Ariel - movie Fri?
5:15	Get pictures online	Math: do 1-10 evens	Check email
5:30			
5:45	Help w/ dinner	Help w/ dinner	Help w/ dinner
6:00	Ask Mom to sign	Ask Dad to edit	Ask Mom Movie Fr?
6:15	forms for music	critique	
6:30	Spanish Poster:	Sci: Rev Flashcards	
6:45	Layout pictures	Take practice quiz	
7:00	Write	9:30 Sci: make	7:00	Karate	9:30
7:15	Sentences	9:45 flashcds	Math: 9:45		9:45
7:30	Glue	10:00	Finish ex 10:00		10:00
7:45	Borders	10:15	His: Rev 10:15		10:15
8:00	History	10:30	flashcds 10:30	Piano practice	10:30
8:15	Flashcds	10:45	Spanish: 10:45		10:45
8:30		11:00	Flashcds 11:00		11:00
8:45	English	11:15	new voc. 11:15	Read	11:15
9:00	rough	11:30	11:30	Eng bk	11:30

Need Help? Call 831.462.5655

Time Management for the Family

Social Time and Down Time

for them to take the time to fill in the rest of the semester when they do get the schedule. It will make adding in due dates for projects and homework much easier.

Social Time and Down Time

Like you, your children need time to unwind, time to be with friends, and time to just be alone. But since children face heavy demands, this need often goes overlooked. Make sure to schedule in some social time and some down time for your kids, otherwise their lives will lose balance and they might get burned out.

One family I know does an excellent job of this. The Mitchells have two children: Ariel is a high achiever who buries herself in academics. Curtis needs lots of reminders to turn off the TV and start on his homework. For Ariel, her parents require her to spend one weekend evening with a friend. To meet this requirement, Ariel blocks off time on Saturday night from dinnertime to bedtime to go to the movies or to have slumber parties. This requires her to shift her homework load to other times. For Curtis, his parents require that all homework be completed before he can watch TV or have a friend over. As a result, Curtis super-organizes his planner so that he will get homework done by Saturday at 3:00 p.m. Then he has the rest of the weekend to play.

Get a Copy of your Children's' Schedule

Once they're done with scheduling, make sure to get a copy of their regular schedule, as well as any special appointments that they have. Put a copy in your planner so that you can stay prepared and coordinated.

Limiting Time-Wasters

Most children have some activity that wastes too much of their time. The most common time-wasters are the telephone, the internet, and the TV. It might be unrealistic for you to completely eliminate these time-

Need Help? Call 831.462.5655

Time Management for the Family

wasters, but it is reasonable for you to make sure your kids find a healthy balance with other activities. This will prevent them from falling into addiction.

If your child is talking on the phone for hours every night, set up rules to limit their phone use. Naturally, homework responsibilities should be the first priority, but allow your child to block off 15 – 30 minutes for phone time at a designated time during the early evening. Many families set phone curfews where kids can't receive phone calls after a certain hour.

Now many kids are spending more and more time online. They might be spending this time gossiping through instant messages or e-mail, just as they do on the phone. Like phone time, you may need to limit the amount of time your child spends online. Or you could reward your children for completing all their tasks by giving them extra time to spend online.

What about Chores?

Children benefit from doing chores or having some type of commitment to help maintain the house and family. These commitments teach them how to be responsible and how to take pride in the upkeep of their home. Whether your child just needs to make his bed or vacuum the house and make two dinners, they will need to block off time to do it. If your child regularly schedule chores into their schedule, you'll have less nagging to do because you'll know they have planned to do it. For more information about scheduling chores, see the chapter titled *Household Chores*.

Sample Planner Page: Scheduling Time For Chores

February 7-13, 2005

Time	Fri., Feb. 7	Sat., Feb. 8	Sun., Feb. 9
7:00	Shower	Shower	Shower
7:30	Breakfast	Breakfast	Breakfast
8:00	Leave for School	Leave for School	Leave for School
8:30	Homeroom	Homeroom	Homeroom
9:00			
9:15	English	History	English
9:30	Finish reading ch 2	Review sheet due	Write critique
9:45			
10:00			
10:15			
10:30			
10:45	Math	Spanish	Math
11:00	pp 35: 1-35 odds	Spanish poster due	pp 37: 1-20 evens
11:15			
11:30			
11:45			
12:00			
12:15	Lunch	Lunch	Lunch
12:30			
12:45			
1:00			
1:15	Science	Music	Science
1:30	Lab writeup due	Turn in forms	Quiz on Ch 2
1:45			
2:00			
2:15			
2:30			
2:45	Dad pick up	Mom picks up	Take bus
3:00	Piano lessons	Chores: trash cans in	Chores: vacuum LR
3:15		His: flashcards	His: Read notes
3:30			Rev flashcards
3:45	Chores: trash out		Rev worksheet
4:00	History worksheet		Take practice quiz
4:15		Eng: Finish critique	Span: Quiz self
4:30		spell check	Write words 10X
4:45			Rev flashcards
5:00	Spanish Poster:		Call Ariel - movie Fri?
5:15	Get pictures online	Math: do 1-10 evens	Check email
5:30			
5:45	Help w/ dinner	Help w/ dinner	Help w/ dinner
6:00	Ask Mom to sign	Ask Dad to edit	Ask Mom Movie Fr?
6:15	forms for music	critique	
6:30	Spanish Poster:	Sci: Rev Flashcards	
6:45	Layout pictures	Take practice quiz	
7:00	Write		Karate
7:15	Sentences	Math:	
7:30	Glue	Finish ex	
7:45	Borders	His: Rev	
8:00	History	flashcds	Piano practice
8:15	Flashcds	Spanish:	
8:30		Flashcds	
8:45	English	new voc	Read
9:00	rough		Eng bk
9:30	Sci: make		
9:45	flashcds		
10:00			
10:15			
10:30			
10:45			
11:00			
11:15			
11:30			

Need Help? Call 831.462.5655

Time Management for the Family

Chapter VII
Weekly Family Meetings

Plan to keep having weekly meetings to keep everyone synchronized. At the meetings you not only discuss one another's schedules, but you can plan and brainstorm for upcoming events, or you can discuss other issues of the family. Not only will they save everyone time, but family meetings also ensure that every family member knows what's going on in everyone else's life, which creates a sense of unity and cohesion that most families lack.

Family Brainstorm Sessions

Family brainstorm sessions allow everyone to be included in family affairs, and they are the most fun part of the family meetings. This is where you can plan events such as vacations, parties, or anything else that the family will do as a whole. Schedule dates to make plans or decisions about future things today. Everyone involved should enter the dates in their planners too. Give yourselves plenty of time in advance to purchase

Weekly Family Meetings

tickets and make reservations. For birthday parties, allow several months to brainstorm about party themes and to purchase all the goodies. But don't start brainstorming during the first family meeting; it will only take the focus off of getting your family organized.

Synchronizing Family Members' Schedules

You need to synchronize family members' schedules so that your days run smoothly and so that one person's miscue doesn't domino into a problem for the entire family. Start by bringing everyone to today's date. As a group, discuss your schedules starting with today. First discuss what you're all going to do for the rest of the day. Then continue to discuss each day for the entire upcoming week.

For instance, you would say, *on Monday, Rob is making dinner so he should thaw out the ingredients for his meal before he goes to work*. Rob then enters this task in the morning before he leaves for work and enters what meal he'll be preparing upon his return that evening. When you say *I'm driving everybody to school*, the children should jot down *mom drives* so they know who will be driving them. If a child has a potluck at school on Monday and needs to bring fruit punch, then they enter *take fruit punch* for Monday morning.

Continue to discuss each day of the week so that everyone can enter in the times they need to know. Since you're the leader in the family's organization, you may want to jot down your children's and your spouse's schedules on the far right side of the daily columns in your planner. As you continue to discuss your schedules during family meetings, the rest of the family will become more familiar with the style and strategy. Eventually, the process will become much quicker.

Need Help? Visit www.meritworld.com

Plan your Weekend

Plan your Weekends or You'll Wonder Where the Time Went!

When you get to the weekend, ask *what's going on this weekend?* Weekends are easy to forget, but that doesn't mean that the kids will be any less busy on them. It's preferable to hear about weekend plans a week in advance so that everyone can adjust their schedules. After one child lists their plans, encourage the others to do so as well.

Everyone should enter each family member's schedule for the weekend so they know who's doing what, when, and where. If you want to have a special family day or night, have everyone block off the time now. Otherwise, don't count on it being available. It's amazing how quickly your time gets zapped if you don't reserve the time in advance.

Coordinate the Shopping Schedule

The family meetings are also a good time to coordinate the shopping schedule. Mention your shopping dates so the children know when you are going out. Run through the current shopping list. Ask if they know of anything else that needs to be bought. Let them know the time when you will need to know their shopping requests. For more details on efficient shopping, see the chapter titled *Managing the Household*.

Plan Your Next Meeting before you Leave

While you still have everyone together, schedule the next family meeting. The rest of the family meetings should take substantially less time than the first one. Make sure that everyone schedules it in their planners. Before you close the meeting, ask if anyone else has anything they need to say.

Need Help? Call 831.462.5655

Weekly Family Meetings

Chapter VIII

Use Trays for Family Communication

In order to keep good communication between all family members throughout in between family meetings, set up stackable trays for every member of the family. You might want to have trays for your household help. Place the trays in a central location where they can be checked on a regular basis. Label each tray with each person's name.

How to Pass Messages with Trays

The trays are used for the members of the family to pass messages to one another. Request that everyone write notes when they have messages for one another and place them in the appropriate person's tray. If you need to relay the same messages to the entire family, make copies and place them in their trays. By placing notes in others' trays, it takes the pressure off of you to remember to relay the message. No longer will you be bickering because an important message never made it to you. No longer will everyone be nagging one another to get things done.

Need Help? Call 831.462.5655

Use Trays for Family Communication

Make Sure Trays Get Checked Regularly

The trays contain important messages, so they need to be checked regularly. Because some family members may neglect to check, place mail and magazines in trays too. That makes the trays an important place for everyone to collect their messages as soon as they walk in the door. Children who don't get much mail might need more motivation to check their trays. You and your spouse can occasionally surprise them with happy little notes. Or you can offer rewards. Try a note like: "If you are checking your tray today, January 7, you can make yourself a bowl of ice cream!" Treats will encourage them to check their trays often.

How to Handle Requests You Find in Your Tray

Notes that family members receive in their trays should be treated like any other task. If you're making a request for a family member to do something, they should enter a time to do it in their planners. Whenever relevant, family members should respond to notes by placing the response in the giver's tray. The response should usually mention when the family member plans to complete the task. You can even enter the expected date of completion into your planner so you can later check up that they did indeed get it done. Children especially need to be reminded to enter these tasks into their planners.

When I want my daughter to gather the plastic bags to take to the grocery store, I place a note in her tray with the request and ask her to put the bag in my car by Monday night. If I have to ask my husband a question about whether or not he paid the tuition for our other daughter's gymnastics, it's easier to just leave a note. He can write *yes* or *no* on the same note and pop it into my tray.

Chapter IX
Cooking Meals

Since we eat several meals every day, cooking has a way of taking up a good chunk of time. Some mothers save time by relying on restaurants and prepared foods, but that can become an expensive and unhealthy habit. That's why you need a plan to make cooking your meals run more efficiently, which will ultimately afford you more time for other things.

Plan the Menu for One Week

Planning a menu will save you time. Always consider what foods you will have in stock. Based on your schedules, decide what you and your family will be eating for each meal of the week, then update the weekly shopping list accordingly. You should plan so that you avoid having to make excess trips to the market.

You can thaw out your ingredients in the morning before you leave for work and start cooking right when you get home. Enter this in your planner so you don't forget.

Need Help? Call 831.462.5655

Cooking Meals

Cook larger batches of food when you do cook. You'll have leftovers to last several days. That way, you're cooking fewer times but getting the same amount of food.

If you know which days you will be especially busy, you can plan not to cook. Don't get stuck buying another fast-food dinner. You can rely on leftovers. Or you can delegate the responsibility for cooking to other family members.

Kids Can Make Their Own Lunches

Children as young as five years old can make their own lunches. When the child prepares their lunch, not only will it save you some time, but they will feel more independent and they won't get stuck at school with a lunch that they don't want to eat.

Give guidelines for the different food groups that need to be included in their lunch. That way they won't just pack junk food. For instance, make sure each lunch includes some fruit or vegetable, a healthy beverage, and a sandwich with protein. It's probably easiest for them to pack foods that come prepackaged or foods that require little preparation, such as leftovers.

Lunches can be prepared the night before while dinner is being cleaned up. That way any mess they make can easily be cleaned up and you won't have to rush to get it made in the morning.

Let the Kids Prepare Individual Meals

You can get away with cooking even fewer meals if you have the kids prepare several of the family meals each week. Kids actually enjoy this chance to be independent and creative. Younger children can be in charge of making simple breakfasts of cereal, waffles, and fresh fruit. The older children can make more complicated dinners. As for busy family members, they

Need Help? Visit www.meritworld.com

Weekly Shopping List and Menu

Week of: _____

Weekly Shopping List and Menu

Weekly Menu

Meal	Sunday	Monday	Tuesday	Wednesday	Thursday	Friday	Saturday
B:							
L:							
D:							

Weekly Shopping List

Vegetables	Fruit	Meat	Frozen Foods
Asparagus	Apples	Beef: ground	Desserts:
Avocados	Bananas	Beef: ribs	Dinners:
Broccoli	Blueberries	Beef: roast	Ice Cream:
Cabbage	Cantaloupe	Beef: short ribs	Juice:
Carrots	Cherries	Beef: steaks	Juice:
Cauliflower	Grapes	Chicken: boneless	Juice:
Celery	Grapefruit	Chicken: breasts	Veg: broccoli
Cucumbers	Lemons	Chicken: legs	Veg: corn
Eggplant	Limes	Chicken: thighs	Veg: mixed veg
Garlic	Mangos	Chicken: whole	Veg: spinach
Ginger	Melons	Chicken: wings	
Green Chilis	Oranges	Deli Meat:	**Dairy**
Green Onions	Pears	Game hens	Butter
Green Peppers	Peaches	Hot Dogs	Cheese:
Lettuce	Pineapples	Lamb: chops	Cheese:
Mushrooms	Plums	Lamb: leg	Cottage Cheese
Onions	Pomegranate	Pork: bacon	Cream
Parsley	Raspberries	Pork: chops	Cream Cheese
Potatoes	Strawberries	Pork: ground	Eggs
Squash	Tangerines	Pork: roast	Margarine
Sprouts		Sausage: breakfst	Milk:
String Beans	**Seasonings**	Sausage: pork	Yogurt:
Tomatoes	Chili Powder	Sausage: turkey	
Zucchini	Garlic Powder	Seafood:	**Drinks**
Liquor	Pepper	Seafood:	Juice:
Beer:	Salt	Turkey: ground	Mixers:
Brandy	Seasoning Salt	Turkey:	Soda:
Wine:	Soy Sauce	Veal: cutlets	
Other:	Vinegar	Veal:	

Need Help? Call 831.462.5655

Cooking Meals

Weekly Shopping List

Packaged Goods	Baking Goods		Canned Goods		Kitchen Supplies
Cereal:	Baking Soda		Fruit: peaches		Coffee Filters
Chocolate	Baking Powder		Fruit: pears		Dish Detergent
Coffee	Cake Mix:		Fruit: pineapple		Dishwasher Det.
Cookies:	Chocolate Chips		Pickles		Foil
Crackers:	Flour		Refried Beans		Freezer Bags
Dried Fruit:	Frosting Mix:		Sauce:		Garbage Bags
Noodles:	Honey		Sauce:		Napkins
Rice:	Nuts		Seafood: clams		Paper Plates
Soups:	Oil:		Seafood: tuna		Paper Towels
Stuffing/Rice	Shortening		Soup:		Plastic Wrap
Tea	Sugar		Soup:		Oven Cleaner
			Veg: beets		Sandwich Bags
	Toiletries		Veg: beans		Trash Bags
Bottled Goods	Conditioner		Veg: corn		
Bar-B-Que Sauce	Cotton Balls		Veg: kidney beans		**Cleaning Supplies**
Cocktail Sauce	Cotton Swabs		Veg: mushrooms		Ammonia
Jam/Jellies:	Dental Floss		Veg: olives		Bleach
Ketchup	Deodorant		Veg: peas		Broom
Mayonnaise	Facial Tissue		Veg: tomatoes		Cleanser
Mustard	Lotion				Bathroom Cleaner
Peanut Butter	Polish/Remover		**Pet Supplies**		Distilled Water
Relish	Razor Blades		Bird Seed		Dust Pan
Salsa	Rubbing Alcohol		Cat Food		Fabric Softener
	Sanitary Napkins		Dog Biscuits		Feather Duster
	Shampoo		Dog Food		Furniture Polish
	Shaving Cream		Fish Food		Handwash Dtgnt.
Bakery	Tampons		Flea Collar		Laundry Detergent
Bread:	Toilet Tissue		Pet Shampoo		Mop Ends
Muffins:	Toothbrush				Rubber Gloves
Pastries:	Toothpaste				Vacuum Bags
Rolls:			**Miscellaneous**		
Tortillas:					

Need Help? Visit www.meritworld.com

can prepare simpler things like salad dressings and marinades on the days when they are less busy.

Your kids will need more help with cooking at first, but once they get the hang of it, they should be able to do it all on their own. It's generally a good idea to let kids cook the same few meals each week until they become very competent and quick at preparation. When they're ready and when you're tired of having the same thing, they can select a new recipe.

Again set meal guidelines so you don't end up getting cold cereal for dinner or pasta for three days in a row. Make sure that the meals chosen give you a healthful variety.

Someone will need to make sure that all of the ingredients for the meals make it onto the shopping list ahead of time. In my family, this responsibility falls on the one who cooks the meal. This person is also in charge of thawing out meats ahead of time, setting the table, and cleaning-up. That way they own the entire process. It makes for less haggling and finger pointing.

Meal Prep as a Family

If the idea of having one child or person responsible for one entire meal doesn't appeal to you, call on the whole family to make dinner together. Of course, you'll need to schedule this at a time that works for everyone. With a few helpers, you may be able to get a well-balanced dinner on the table in under fifteen minutes. If you have enough space, multitask. One family member could prepare each dish, while the youngest could set the table and pour the drinks.

Meal Cleanup

Make sure that your family knows exactly how your cleanup system works and whose responsibility it is. Stipulate it in advance if you want the table cleared,

Cooking Meals

dishes washed, the leftovers put in the fridge, and the table wiped down. This way you'll avoid nagging or doing it yourself.

Chapter X
Household Chores

Even after you've gotten your schedule and your family's schedule in check, it's easy to overlook all the little household chores that need to be done regularly. They don't seem like a lot of work, but if you just ignore them, they pile up and become overwhelming. So make a regular schedule for taking care of household chores. A clean and orderly house not only makes your life more peaceful, but it also lets you use your time more efficiently. Things run smoother and quicker when you aren't constantly digging through clutter looking for things you've lost.

Delegate, Delegate, Delegate!

Traditionally, the bulk of the work of keeping up the house has fallen on the mother—but today it's more realistic for everyone to chip in, especially with so many mothers pursuing active lives outside of the home. If you don't have the time for all the household chores, you can delegate them to other family members.

Need Help? Call 831.462.5655

Household Chores

Often times, mothers think it's easier just to do the job themselves, because at least it gets done right. That may be true, but if your children or spouse can be shown how to do the job nearly as well as you do it, then it's probably a good idea for them to do it. If you do all the work, your children will falsely assume that the household just naturally runs smoothly, giving them an unrealistic picture of how the world works. But when they help out, they learn to appreciate the hard work that goes into keeping up a house. I noticed that my children were more careful about not spilling juice on the refrigerator shelves after they had to clean the refrigerator themselves.

Make a list of chores that the children must do, before they go to school, when they return from school, and before bedtime. If you like beds made and jammies put away before you leave in the morning, make that a rule! Then make a list of all the chores that need to be done on a regular basis. You'll have to decide what's important, and then delegate tasks. You'll be surprised at how much the rest of your family can help you to manage the house—even little children.

What your Kids can do to Help

Before you assign your children chores, consider their ages. Small children (ages 2 – 4) can't be depended on for help with cooking or heavy cleaning, but you can teach them many skills that will make other people's jobs easier. If you organize their bedrooms so that everything has a proper place, you can teach even toddlers how to put things back in where they belong when they're done using them. For instance, certain toys might be stored on particular shelves and different types of clothing might go in different drawers. They can even help with laundry by sorting their clothes by colors, and they can put away some of their own laundry. Small children can also collect laundry baskets and take them to the laundry room and they can collect trash cans throughout the house and dump them into the outside

Need Help? Visit www.meritworld.com

How to Divide up Chores

garbage cans. Although it's easier and quicker for you to put things away yourself, in the long run it'll be much more beneficial for your children to learn to help out.

Elementary school-aged children (5 – 10 years old) can be completely in charge of maintaining their own bedrooms and sorting their own laundry, as well as some of the weekly cleaning responsibilities. They can dust the furniture and water the house plants. By the time they turn 8, children have the coordination to vacuum floors and to strip down beds.

Middle school-aged children (11 – 13 years old) are ready and eager to be independent. They can do laundry, fold clothes, change sheets, shake out rugs, vacuum stairs, clean the refrigerator, and sweep the floors.

High school-aged young adults (14 – 18 years old) are capable of (although not always agreeable to) doing almost anything that needs to be done to maintain the house. Your high school child can do more difficult tasks that younger children can't, such as cleaning the oven and microwave, replacing light bulbs, washing windows, cleaning bathrooms, mopping floors, and washing dishes.

How to Divide Up Chores

Begin with a list of chores that need to be done on a regular basis. Figure out how often it needs to be done—whether it's daily, weekly, or monthly. Estimate how long each chore will take. Then consider if there are a certain chore that are too complicated for younger children to do.

Looking at the list, try to divide chores up so that everyone has a fairly equal set of responsibilities. Otherwise, your children will be quick to complain that someone's doing an unfair amount of work. If you have children of very different ages, dividing up the chores

Need Help? Call 831.462.5655

Household Chores

might be tough. But if everyone is fairly equal in abilities, you might divide the chores as follows: (1) clean kitchen; (2) vacuum, sweep and mop; (3) dust, take out trash and recycling; and (4) clean bathrooms.

Assign the Chores

The most convenient time to assign chores is during a family meeting. Plan a set time that everyone can fit into their schedules. If one of your children has a baseball schedule that changes every week, plan the housecleaning times around the games. Make sure that the children block off enough time to get their chores done. For the first weeks they do a chore, allow a little extra time to coach the kids on their jobs.

Rotate the Jobs

Rotate the jobs each week. This gives everyone the opportunity to learn how to do all of the various tasks needed to maintain a clean house. Once the family gets a taste for the different tasks, ask them which tasks they prefer doing. You'll also notice that certain people do certain jobs better than others, and hopefully, assigning permanent tasks will be easy for you. If it looks like a battle to decide who does what, alternate the desired tasks. Or you may need to reevaluate why everybody wants one particular task. It may just be that it is the easiest task.

Spring Cleaning Day

Does your house need some major cleaning or reorganization? Maybe the outside of the house needs some maintenance or the yard needs some landscaping work. Enlist the family by making it a group project where everyone does a portion of the work. I recommend planning ahead to set aside one day on the weekend for the entire family to Spring-clean the house. That way, it feels more like a team effort.

Need Help? Visit www.meritworld.com

How to Divide the Jobs

When my family Spring-cleans, first we list all of the things that we think need to be done. After writing out a list, I ask who would like to do each task. Everyone calls out the tasks they want to do. After a little haggling over the unpleasant tasks, such as turning the compost or hand-washing the light fixtures, the jobs are all claimed. Next, we decide when we'll all do the tasks.

Discuss how long everyone thinks their task will take and block it off in your appointment books. You may need to divide the cleaning dates up into several days over a few weeks to allow enough time to get the more involved projects done.

Getting the Spring Cleaning Supplies

Before closing your planners, ask each person what supplies their job will require. Add any supplies you don't already have to your shopping list, and make sure to pick them up before the cleaning is scheduled to begin. For instance, if you'd like to start the new flower garden but you need to weed, sow, and fertilize the soil, make sure you have everything you need ahead of time— such as gloves, garden tools, fertilizers, topsoil, mulch, and seeds. If you don't have everything you need in advance, then you run into one of two problems: either you give up, or you waste your time by running last-minute errands.

Spring-Cleaning Day Itself

When the day actually comes, I try to make it as exciting as possible. I crank up the stereo and order the family a pizza. I go around and check up that the kids are doing their jobs properly. Of course, younger children will need more guidance, but teenagers can be quite stubborn. Once the day is over, everyone will feel better about how nice the house looks, especially since so much of their sweat went into it.

Need Help? Call 831.462.5655

Household Chores

Chapter XI
Shopping and Errands

How much time do you spend running errands? Probably too much. If you're like most people, you probably head to the store whenever you run out of something, which means that you end up at the store several times a week, or maybe even several times a day. If you do this, you waste a tremendous amount of time—driving to the store, parking your car, searching the shelves, grabbing the impulse buys, waiting in long lines, loading your car, driving back home, and finally unloading your car. But if you plan ahead, you can streamline your errands to save time.

Only Buy Groceries once a Week

If you resolve to only shop for groceries once per week, your life becomes much more efficient. You'll notice that you have more free time since you're not running to the market every day, and you'll also notice that grocery bills are lower, because the family learns not to eat food so quickly.

Shopping and Errands

Set a regular day of the week when you will do your weekly grocery shopping. Let all the family members know in advance which day of the week it is that you plan to shop. Tell them that you're not going to go off schedule, so if they miss the time, then they'll have to wait until next week. This schedule might seem harsh at first, but if you stick with it, they'll soon adapt.

Use a Grocery List

With a list, you don't have the burden of remembering everything once you're at the grocery store and you're less tempted to buy food out of impulse. Keep a grocery list posted on the fridge throughout the week so that your family can easily add to it. Whenever someone uses up some food item, they should add it to the grocery list. That way you'll know to replenish it. See Page 69-70.

Before you leave to go shopping, double-check the list. Make sure that all staple foods are included as well as ingredients for the meals planned for the week. Ask the family if there are any last minute requests.

Plan out the Meals for the Week

In order to shop only once per week, you'll need to plan out meals for the entire week. With the meals pre-planned, much of your weekly grocery-shopping list can be easily determined. All you need to do is fill in the ingredients needed for each meal. If you are indecisive or your family has picky eaters, let different family members plan out meals for certain days.

Driving Errands

Your schedule can also be made more efficient by coordinating the places and the days that you run driving errands. Designate certain days for running errands in certain parts of town. Otherwise you could end up driving back and forth to the same parts of town several times

Need Help? Visit www.meritworld.com

Take Advantage of your Commute

a week, which wastes time and gas. Once you schedule your errands, enter them in your planner.

Enter the store name in your appointment book so you know what errands you'll be running during the blocked out time. If you have more than one location listed, number the locations based on the most convenient order. Consider traffic, store hours, and whether the items are perishable. Make sure you block off enough driving time.

Take Advantage of your Commute

If you can pack in an errand that's near your work on your lunch hour, you're really using your time efficiently. If you need to run errands that are not near work, set up time on the way home from work or on the weekends to do them.

One mother I know takes advantage of her commute by using it to run errands that are right along the route. She uses her lunch break on Tuesdays to run errands that are near her work. On her way home on Thursdays, she stops at the stores that are nearer to her home. Then she buys groceries on Sundays, since the grocery store is out of the way of her commute. This means that she has four days where she is free of running any errands.

Don't do it all Yourself

If you feel like you're doing more driving than you want, delegate some of the errands to other family members. If your teenager is old enough to drive, they can help out with running errands and transporting younger children. Your spouse may be able to pick up some of the errands. You could even ask your spouse about changing their schedule to make things easier on you.

Need Help? Call 831.462.5655

Shopping and Errands

Have it Delivered

Save time by having items shipped to you from a catalogue or an online market. Nowadays, almost anything can be ordered off the internet. Although you may pay extra for shipping, you save shopping time and driving time, not to mention gas money. You also get a better price because you can comparison-shop.

Chapter XII
Time for You!

Schedule Time for YOU!

Although it is one of the most important tasks to schedule, it is the one most often forgotten—time for you! With all your responsibilities to others, you are probably the first to sacrifice your free time in when there's an emergency. But we all need time to be alone and relax. Mothers especially deserve it, since we work so hard. You may need a massage or a swim. How about a bike ride or a little hike? You could peruse the bookstore or read some poetry.

Whether you need 30 minutes a day or three hours on the weekend, block it off in your planner. If you don't block it off in advance, the time could easily be taken up by something else. If your home is too small or too hectic to afford you the space to relax, schedule your "you" time at a location away from the house and free of interruptions.

Need Help? Call 831.462.5655

Time for You!

Creative Time for You

Having a creative outlet is often overlooked, but it can add a sense of balance and accomplishment to your life. A creative outlet is especially important if you feel stifled by the repetition and thanklessness of being a mother. For those with an artistic side, schedule time to work on an art project or to take art classes. Others could write a book or work on a garden. Maybe you want to learn to tango or start doing yoga. You might think that there's no way you'll ever find time, but you'll be surprised how much you really can squeeze in if you use the planner.

Time to get Perspective

With all the day-to-day runaround it's easy to lose perspective on your life and where it's headed. That's why it's important to use some of your "you" time to reflect on your life as a whole. You can re-evaluate your personal relationships, the development of your children, and the path of your career. By contemplating these issues ahead of time, you avoid running into last minute crises later.

Chapter XIII

Other Ways to Better Use your Time

Once you get on a roll with time management, it's hard to stop. In this chapter, we'll continue with some odds-and-ends that don't fit into the other chapters. These little secrets will make your days run even smoother.

Review Your Planner Entries for Better Time Management

After a few months on the time management program, check back with your planner to re-evaluate how useful it has been and how realistically you have been using it. This is time to get perspective on how the time management program has been working for you.

Look at the past weeks. Are you highlighting everything? When you do more tasks than you originally planned, have you still been entering in those tasks and highlighting them off? Have you been over-scheduling yourself? Have you been playing catch-up or have you

Other Ways to Better Use your Time

constantly been rescheduling missed tasks? Does your schedule realistically reflect how you've actually been using your time? It's easy to set an ambitious schedule, but it's harder to follow it.

Things rarely run perfectly at first, so don't get discouraged if you notice problems. Once you identify the problems, you can easily take steps to readjust. It's possible that you have been under-estimating how much time tasks take, or maybe you've just been procrastinating or getting distracted.

Don't be a Slave to Your Phone!

You'll find that you are more productive when you have a plan to control how to use the phone. If you use the phone a lot, you should schedule two blocks of time each day to get your calls done all at once. Otherwise, you're living at the mercy of when the phone happens to ring and when you happen to remember to call, which means that your stretches of productivity are constantly being interrupted.

You should designate certain times for phone calls. Make sure that those who might need to contact you know these times. In other words, you might plan to receive phone calls between 1:00 – 1:30 p.m., which is when you're already planning to do light tasks like reading your mail and checking your e-mail. Then if they call, you aren't seriously disrupted. At all other times, avoid the interruption by either letting the call go to voice-mail or by screening your calls.

When you call others, often you're better off just leaving a detailed message for the recipient than to actually talk to them directly. Talking directly is useful when you need to collaborate, but we too often we get sidetracked with chitchat. When leaving messages that may require a callback, mention the times you're available in order to avoid phone tag.

Need Help? Visit www.meritworld.com

E-mail is Fast and Effective

Using e-mail is generally more efficient than using the phone, so try to use e-mail whenever possible. E-mail has several advantages. You avoid wasting your time playing phone tag. Confrontational situations and dreaded callbacks can be handled more diplomatically. In addition, you have a permanent record of your correspondences. E-mail also improves communication and decision making, because you can articulate your concerns with careful precision. Just make sure you aren't checking your e-mail every five minutes, because that will eat up lots of time.

Setting your Limits

It's too easy to get trapped into giving up your time for other people's friendly requests. When a parent asks you go to their child's play or when a co-worker asks you to do some of their work, think about whether you really have the time. You're doing yourself little good by being a pushover. Decide your priorities and assert yourself. When asked to volunteer your time, remember that you have the ultimate authority to say no, and you don't have to feel guilty. You can always politely say that under different circumstances, you would be glad to say yes, but that because of your schedule and your family's schedule, you have to say no.

Need Extra Help?

Maybe you've done everything possible, but your energy is wearing thin and you still don't have enough time to take care of all your demands. If you can afford it, it might be time to hire outside help. You can hire someone to help out with childcare, cleaning, cooking, errands, chores, or driving. The cost might be worth it. Just make sure that you leave yourself some meaningful time to spend with your children.

Need Help? Call 831.462.5655

Other Ways to Better Use your Time

Limiting Time-Wasters

We all have some habit that wastes too much of our time. The most common time-wasters are the telephone, the internet, and the TV. It might be unrealistic for you to completely eliminate these time-wasters, but it is reasonable for you to find a healthy balance. You could schedule in a limited amount of time for them, or you could schedule these sorts of activities as rewards at the end of the day for completing everything that you had scheduled.

If that still doesn't work, you might find ways to eliminate the temptation while you're working. To prevent yourself from wasting your time online, work in a place where there is no computer around or use a laptop and take it where there is no internet connection. If you go to a library or coffee shop, you can escape the temptations of the TV and the telephone.

Being More Efficient at Work

The office has its own set of distractions to deal with. If co-workers are always coming by your office for chitchat, re-arrange your office so you can't make eye contact with them as they walk by. That way, they'll be less likely to interrupt you. If you have fewer distractions at home than at the office, try to arrange to do more of your work from home. Or you could restructure your day so that you tackle bigger projects at times in the day when fewer co-workers are around to distract you. If the phone is a distraction, you can have the secretary or the voice-mail prevent calls from bothering you when you're busy.

Teach Time Management to Your Co-workers

Perhaps you work at an office where the disorganization of your co-workers causes problems for you too. If so, you might want to look into teaching your co-workers what you've learned about time

Need Help? Visit www.meritworld.com

Teach Time Management to Your Co-Workers

management. By teaching them these skills, you'll find that your workplace will also run smoother, which will not only make things better for the company—but also for you.

Of course, unless you're the one running the place, you probably can't impose time management on your co-workers. You may need to get the time management plan approved by the powers that be. Many managers would enthusiastically welcome a plan to improve productivity. In fact, your initiative and enthusiasm to improve the office might even earn you praise or advancement.

Proceed one department at a time. You could start with the department that is known for being the most disorganized and behind schedule. Or you could start at the lower levels of the bureaucracy and work your way up.

Organize a first meeting to teach them how to use the planners to plan their individual jobs and projects. The principle is the same for your office planning as it is for you and your family. Everyone will need their own planner, and everyone should be assigned a stackable tray. Synchronize your schedules in the way that works best. Use your planners to schedule business and company functions, such as luncheons, meetings, and business trips. Consider deadlines and long-term goals. After the meeting, check up that everyone is entering deadlines in their appointment books and blocking off time to do the projects.

Other Ways to Better Use your Time

Chapter XIV
A Word on Motivation

When you first get started on this time management program, it's tempting to feel overwhelmed and to start neglecting your planner. Of course it's a big change and it's a lot to learn. That's why you'll need to find a way to keep yourself motivated. In this section, I'll offer some suggestions. But since sources of motivation vary from person to person, you'll have to discover what works best for you.

Don't Go it Alone

Have someone else start the program alongside you. It could be other family members or it could be another mother. Making this big change alone can feel daunting, especially if you've tried something similar before. But with others alongside you, you have more of a support network. You can discuss common challenges, you can give one another helpful advice, and you can praise one another for your successes. The resolution becomes easier to keep when you have the support,

A Word on Motivation

encouragement, and compassion of other people in the same situation.

Think about How Much You've Changed

If you're like me, you'll be motivated by the sheer joy of the feelings of accomplishment and control. It feels great to get the most out of every moment of your day. Just think how things have improved! You're a better provider for your family, and you have the free time to relax by yourself or to enjoy with your family. If you just stop and contemplate how much things have improved, it will help you to stick with the time management program.

Think back on how chaotic and overwhelming your life used to be. Remember the feelings of being out of control? Remember feeling like you got nothing done all day? Remember feeling like there was a mountain of tasks towering over your every moment? Now think about the prospect of returning to this chaos. That alone should make you want to stick with the time management program.

Treat Yourself

Give yourself a more tangible reward too from time to time. Reward yourself for each week or month that you stay with the time management program. You could go out for a nice dinner, or you could get yourself something you've always wanted. Spending a little time by yourself can be just as rewarding as something tangible. For more on this, see the chapter titled *Time for You!*

Kids Especially Need Motivation

If your kids are also using the planner, think about how you're going to motivate them. Motivation is so important with children, because they will have a hard time appreciating how the planner is helpful. Children

Kids Especially Need Motivation

focus more on the short term. They just want to run around and play or do whatever it is they feel like doing. For that reason, they might see the planner as more of a chore.

Reward those who efficiently use their planners. Give them plenty of praise, and make sure to set a good example by using your own planner. Think about what it is that your kids really want. You could take them out to dinner, you could let them have a movie night with friends, or you could buy them that toy they've always wanted. Reward them regularly for every week, month, or year that they successfully use the planner. Let them know that they should not expect the reward as a matter of course, but only if they use their planner as you showed them.

A Word on Motivation

Conclusion

    Now you're ready to take the first big step in taking back control of your life. Start by using the planner for your personal or business tasks and then gradually add your family's activities, chores, and other tasks. I have found that one of the best ways to stay organized and to consistently use the planner is to teach others how to use it. By explaining how to use it and guiding others to stay on task, you'll become even more efficient yourself.

    The most exciting part about using the planner is that you'll actually find that you have more free time to do the things you really want to do. Now, get going! Open up the Merit Planner and start entering in your tasks!

Need Help? Call 831.462.5655

Index

A

after-School Activities 50, 52, 54
appointment books 52, 77, 89

B

brainstorm 33, 61, 62
business 23, 28, 89, 95

C

calendar 12, 18, 43
career 7, 28, 84
carpool 44
childcare 87
chores 17, 58, 73, 74, 75, 76, 87, 95
cleaning 49, 71, 74, 75, 76, 77, 87
communication 65, 87
commute 23, 81
computerized organizers 12
cooking 18, 49, 67, 68, 71, 74, 87

D

delegate 68, 73, 74, 81
distractions 88
driving 18, 44, 49, 62, 79, 80, 81, 82, 87

E

e-mail 58, 86, 87, 88
errands 17, 18, 49, 77, 79, 80, 81, 87

F

family meetings 51, 61, 62, 63, 65

G

goals 17, 27, 30, 89

H

handheld electronic organizers 15
highlight 36, 41, 42, 85
homework 19, 49, 50, 52, 53, 54, 57, 58

I

instant messages 58

J

journal 17, 18

L

lunch 18, 23, 49, 68, 81, 89

M

menu 15, 67
Merit Planner 12, 15, 95
message 58, 65, 66, 86
motivation 42, 66, 91, 92

N

notes section 33

P

party 49, 50, 52, 62
projects 17, 28, 33, 41, 53, 54, 57, 77, 88, 89

R

restructure 88

S

shopping 23, 50, 63, 67, 71, 77, 79, 80, 82
synchronize 61, 62, 89

T

time-wasters 57, 88
trays 12, 65, 66

Need Help? Call 831.462.5655

www.ingramcontent.com/pod-product-compliance
Lightning Source LLC
LaVergne TN
LVHW011428080426
835512LV00005B/325